Vernacular Architecture of Fingal

AN ILLUSTRATED SURVEY

Brendan P Lynch

Published by
Brendan P Lynch
www.brendanplynch.com

ISBN 978-0-9555711-0-7

This publication has received support from the Heritage Council
under the 2007 Publications Grant Scheme.

Important Notice:
The buildings featured in this publication, the majority of which still exist within the
Fingal area, are all private property. No building or site should be entered without prior
permission from the owners.

Set in Sabon Roman

Design and layout by Martin Keaney
www.keaneydesign.ie

Printed by GraphyCems

Contents

Foreword

Vernacular architecture, or traditional structures, have been a characteristic of the Irish landscape for as long as people have inhabited this island. The traditional cottage as regularly featured on postcards still exists, but for decades now a decline in this form of architecture has been under way. Factors influencing the disappearance and slow ruination of these structures include: the last occupant dies and no one is willing or interested in continuing to live in the dwelling; the occupant emigrates, as was often the case in the past; or the occupant builds a new, modern dwelling that they feel offers them a better lifestyle.

However, there is hope – with the growing realisation that vernacular structures do have historical and heritage values, and when refurbished and reused can provide comfortable living conditions. Local authorities such as those in Fingal, Donegal, Clare and Kildare have planning policies that encourage the reuse of vernacular structures – from the modest urban dwelling to the larger farmstead. Fingal County Council's policies are, by far, superior in this regard to those of any other local authority.

Fingal County Council has just commissioned a survey of all its vernacular farmsteads and it is hoped to place a representative sample on its Record of Protected Structures. The remaining county councils across Ireland would do well to follow this example as it is only through sound, comprehensive surveying that the extent to which vernacular structures still exist can be quantified, and from such surveys that planning policies can be formed.

Vernacular structures should be viewed as a resource, not a liability, by the people of Ireland and our planners, and by the developers who have consigned many a fine vernacular structure to the landfill in the pursuit of short-term profits.

This book offers just a brief glimpse into the world of vernacular architecture within a small but significant region of Ireland known as Fingal. It is to be hoped that the book will stimulate more debate on vernacular architecture and, above all, enlighten the reader on the value of this finite and disappearing resource.

Vernacular dwelling, Ballisk, Donabate.

Corrugated iron roofed farm dwelling, Balrickard.

Glossary & Definitions

Architectural Conservation Area (ACA): An area containing structures of special architectural, historical, archaeological, cultural, technical, scientific or social interest or value and which can be specified within a Development Plan as an ACA.

Blades: Roof timbers that are the hewn timbers of a tree. Also known as un-milled timbers.

Bressamers: Large hewn timbers that support the hearth canopy. Rarely to be found in an existing vernacular structure outside of a folk park, some examples are to be found in the Fingal region.

Collar: The horizontal roof timbers that are secured to the blades for support.

Department of the Environment heritage and local government (DOEHLG): This is the government department whose function is to advise formulate and enforce any legislation and policies in the areas of the environment, heritage and local government.

Development Plan (DP): A Development Plan is a plan setting out the overall strategy for proper planning and sustainable development, indicating the development objectives for the area of the planning authority. Development plans must be made every six years. Draft Development Plan (DDP) is this plan in draft form before ratification by the elected representatives.

Direct Entry: As its name suggests the chimney is at either gable end of the structure enabling direct entry without having to negotiate a jam wall.

Dresser: The dresser was a unique piece of Irish vernacular furniture and its primary role was the storage and display of kitchenware.

Fingal County Council (FCC): FCC is the local authority that administers the area known as Fingal.

Gabled: Refers to the vertical triangular piece of the end of a ridged roof from the level of the eaves to the apex.

Hearth Canopy: This refers to the complete structure of the hearth and chimney found in the hearth/kitchen room of a vernacular structure. The hearth canopy is usually situated centrally within the vernacular structure; is very large at the floor level (up to half the width of the structure) and it can be constructed of stone or wattle and clay or all three.

Hipped: In Irish vernacular buildings a hip or hipped roof is one with four sloping surfaces. On a half-hip roof the inclined edges extending down from the ends of the ridge do not reach eaves level.

Jam Wall: The screen wall between entrance and hearth in a lobby-entry vernacular structure. The jam wall is a distinctive feature of vernacular structures and occurs in structures throughout the Fingal region. The jam wall can be constructed of either panelled wood or of clay as part of the hearth canopy.

Lobby Entry: Typically from outside the front door and chimney are in line and on entering the structure one has to negotiate a patrician wall, which usually contains a spy window.

National Inventory of Architectural Heritage (NIAH): The NIAH is a state initiative under the administration of the DOEHLG and whose primary role is to systematically record and publish sample surveys of post 1700 architecture and its associated fixtures and fittings.

Record of Protected Structures (RPS): This is a list drawn up by a local authority of structures which it deems are worthy of protection under part IV of the Planning and Development Act 2000. The list is contained within the written statement of the Development Plan.

Settle Bed: A traditional Irish vernacular piece of furniture usually found within the hearth room. It comprises of a long rectangular seat/bench with a high back. The seat folds out to form a high-sided floor level bed within which a person or persons sleep. By day it is a seat by night it is a bed. It developed from the settle seat found throughout England but the settle bed is only found within Ireland.

Spy Window: A small square or rectangular window found in a hearth wall in the entrance hall of vernacular buildings. As its name suggests it enabled the occupier of the structure to look from the fire hearth canopy, through the window and directly out the front door, to observe approaching visitors.

Thatch: An organic grown material used as a roof covering, examples of which are Oaten Straw, Barley, Water Reed, Flax or Wheat.

Townland: Refers to the smallest administrative territorial unit in Ireland, averaging about half a square mile.

Wattle: An ancient construction technique using interwoven branches or sally rods reinforced with mud or clay.

Whitewash: A mixture of powdered lime and water forming a thick liquid substance used to coat the outer and inner wall surfaces of vernacular structures.

N

Balscadden

BALBRIGGAN

Naul

Balrothery

SKERRIES

Garristown

Damastown

Loughshinny

M1   N1

Oldtown   Ballyboughal

LUSK   RUSH

Donaghmore

Portrane

Rolestown

DONABATE

Lambay
Island

Kilsallaghan

SWORDS

N2

MALAHIDE

Knocksedan

Cloughran

Dublin
Airport

St Margaret's

PORTMARNOCK

Ward

Kinsealy

M50

MULHUDDART

Baldoyle

Finglas   Santry

BLANCHARDSTOWN

Railway

HOWTH

Clonsilla

Royal Canal

DUBLIN
CITY

River Liffey

Introduction

"The built vernacular heritage occupies a central place in the affection and pride of all peoples... It appears informal, but nevertheless orderly. It is utilitarian and at the same time possesses remarkable beauty. It is a focus of contemporary life and at the same time a record of the history of society. It would be unworthy of the heritage of man if care is not taken to conserve these traditional harmonies which constitute the core of mans own existence." (UNESCO, Charter on the built vernacular heritage, Mexico 1999)

Since the first settlers appeared in Mount Sandel, County Derry about 6000 BC, the buildings that have housed the peoples of this island have evolved and developed. Various buildings and their remains from all periods of Irish history dot our landscape and form a vital part of our heritage. Every county in Ireland possesses unique structures and sites that have acquired a character and a cultural significance over time. The buildings we see around us in our villages, towns and cities, and within our rural landscape, have been built to adapt to their particular surroundings. Regional variations in design, structure and the type of materials used are as diverse as the regions' variations in dialect and culture. A traditional house of the Inishowen peninsula will vary significantly from a two-storey smuggler's house found in Rush.

All of these variations are important and we have a duty to ensure that they are conserved, both sympathetically and in a sustainable way, keeping as many of the original features as possible. Our architectural heritage consists not only of houses of artistic merit but also the everyday works of local craftsmen of the past. It is this traditional, or vernacular, architecture which has suffered greatly over the past few decades and is in danger of disappearing from our landscape forever.

Conserving the vernacular architecture of Fingal for the future

Fingal is an area covering 450 square kilometres (173 square miles) of north county Dublin. The name Fingal dates back approximately one thousand years and translates as 'the land of the fair-haired stranger'. The area is both urban and rural. The north of the county, from Dublin airport to north of Balbriggan, is predominantly a rural, agricultural hinterland and this is reflected in the wealth of vernacular structures still in existence.

Postbox in a gate pillar at Damastown (demolished recently).

The area is steeped in local traditions and culture (music, song and dance) which are a part of the vernacular heritage. While the music, song and dance have gone from strength to strength, the vernacular building heritage has been neglected and is disappearing from the landscape at an alarming rate. Each vernacular structure still in existence is a vital part of the area's built heritage. These structures, which are found in both rural and urban settlements, are an asset and should be viewed and treated as such.

The Fingal County Council Draft Development Plan (FCC DDP) of 2005-2011 has specific policies relating to vernacular architecture and, while these policies are to be welcomed, they exist without any comprehensive survey of the area to identify worthy structures for inclusion in the Fingal County Council Record of Protected Structures (FCC RPS). Such a survey is a necessary cornerstone upon which the survival of various examples of vernacular structures (not only dwellings) might be secured for the future.

The National Inventory of Architectural Heritage

The National Inventory of Architectural Heritage (NIAH) carries out sample surveys of Ireland's historical architecture on a county-by-county basis. In the year 2000 the NIAH carried out a sample survey of Fingal's architecture. In total, 659 structures of importance were recorded and of these 85 structures of vernacular interest, 54 vernacular buildings (most of which are on the current thatched dwellings listed in the RPS) and a further 31 cast iron water pumps were identified. With the exception of two cast iron water pumps in the village of Donabate, no other pumps are afforded protection by inclusion in the FCC RPS. The main aim of the NIAH is to identify structures for inclusion in the relevant

Dwelling at Schoolhouse Lane, Corduff, identified in NIAH survey which is also on FCC RPS.

local authority's RPS. Structures identified by the NIAH and listed as 'Regional' or higher are supposed to be included in the local authority's RPS. The 31 cast iron water pumps identified by the NIAH survey of Fingal in 2000 are all rated Regional. Surprisingly, the NIAH managed to miss sixty-seven corrugated iron-over-thatch roofed structures – surely they could have identified one or even two?

This book, which does not claim to be an exhaustive survey, looks at particular examples of vernacular architecture in Fingal. It considers their construction and uses, and their current state of repair (or disrepair). It also notes some specific cases of the failure of the planning authority to protect these structures.

I hope it will both interest and inform those who care about their local heritage.

Brendan P. Lynch

October 2007

Construction Materials

As vernacular buildings decay they often allow the researcher the opportunity to study the materials from which they were constructed. Because vernacular buildings are mainly constructed of organic and natural materials, once they begin to decay they return to the earth from which they were constructed. Today it is still possible to see clay structures on the landscape of Fingal, sticking up like giant termite mounds as their clay walls slowly dissolve back into the soil.

The wattle canopy shown below and the ruined chimney stack both show the most widespread materials used in the construction of vernacular buildings in Fingal – limestone, clay and timber.

Above: many of the older vernacular structures within Fingal are constructed of clay. Often other materials such as bits of pottery were included to prevent rats from borrowing through. Below: a broken piece of a plate within a clay wall.

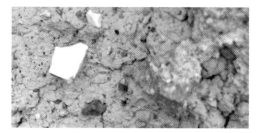

Thatched Structures

"Vernacular architecture accounts for the greater part of the built environment in Ireland. The Irish cultural landscape displays a variety of forms and materials, which can still be defined as traditional or vernacular... traditional conjures up instant mental pictures of thatched, whitewashed and picturesque dwellings. In the context of conservation, thatch and most often the thatched house have been the defining element of what is vernacular. Indeed thatch is considered the most important aspect and sometimes the only one, which receives financial support for conservation."
(Mullane, F. The Heritage of Ireland. Vernacular Architecture. Collins Press 2000)

Fingal still retains forty-four thatched dwellings (as listed in FCC DDP 2005-2011) and an additional sixty-seven (with corrugated iron-over-thatch) identified by the author in a recent pilot survey. This actually means that in 2007 there are at least one hundred and eleven thatched structures. Note 'structures' and not 'dwellings', as some vernacular structures are outbuildings, such as an important example of corrugated iron-over-thatch seen in the forge in the townland of Dallyhaysy, near Balbriggan.

In 1986 Micheal Higgingbottom, of the Office of Public Works, carried out a survey of thatched structures in the Fingal area. The survey identified eighty-six individual thatched structures and was responsible for the listing of some of these structures in the early 1990s. These now constitute the current stock of protected thatched dwellings in Fingal. The present day figure of forty-four protected thatched structures represents a decrease of almost fifty percent since Higgingbottom's survey. This indicates a steady decline in thatched roofs and in some cases the entire structure, but not in all cases as just the roof covering has been removed. With each passing year some dwellings are falling into decay as their elderly occupants pass away.

An estimate by the author of the possible number of thatched structures in Fingal is as follows:

Thatched Structures	44
Corrugated Iron-Over-Thatch	67
Corrugated Iron Only (once thatched)	59
Possible number of thatched structures	**170**

Thatching materials and methods

Thatch as a roof covering was used because it was a by-product of the annual harvest. Of course, as the crop grown varied, so did the material used to re-thatch the roofs of thatched structures. The three types of straw used in the thatching of roofs in Fingal were Wheaten straw, Oaten straw and Barley straw.

The method of thatching employed in the Fingal region is known as Sliced Thatch. Two of the last full-time thatchers, who were responsible between them for thatching the entire stock of thatched roofs in the Fingal area, were the late Charlie Fanning and the late Christy Brereton. Both of these Master Thatchers worked with Oaten straw using the Sliced Thatch method.

Two dwellings from Higgingbottom's survey: (right) a thatched house at Corduff that still stands and (below) a thatched house at Balrothery, now demolished.

Right: Christy Brereton and Christy Jnr, thatching at Rush in 1996 and, below, Charlie Fanning thatching at Skerries in 1980.

The thatcher's tools: slice, hammer, shears, thatching needle, fork, rake, knife.

A ridge made by Christy Brereton before placing on the roof of Brendan P Lynch's refurbished thatched dwelling at Skerries Road, Rush in 1996.

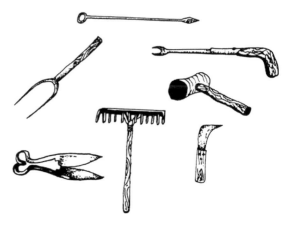

Dwellings

Vernacular dwellings make up by far the majority of vernacular architecture still in existence in the Fingal area. The Irish vernacular dwelling, no matter of which province, is usually rectangular in shape and, while its length may vary according to the prosperity of its original owners, its width is that of its interior room.

In Fingal the characteristics of the vernacular dwelling vary according to location. On the east coast of Fingal, in particular in the towns of Rush and Skerries, the vernacular dwelling is gabled. Usually it has a three- or four-bayed front (ie, it has a main entrance door flanked on either side by widows) usually two on one side and one on the other. An interesting feature in the Rush and Lusk vernacular is the small window in the gable which allows limited light into an upstairs room. This room, of very small proportions, was usually a child's bedroom accessed by a narrow and steep stairs which sometimes was concealed by a tongue and grooved door.

As you move inland to Swords and the villages of Lusk, Donabate, Naul, Garristown, Ballyboughal, Oldtown and the surrounding rural hinterland the dwellings are hipped in form.

A four-bayed dwelling in Rush before renovation, note the small gable window.

Drishogue Lane – (left) a thatched hipped dwelling before refurbishment and (right) after refurbishment, and (below) the two other thatched dwellings.

Drishogue Lane near the village of Ballyboughal has three examples of thatched hipped dwellings. Two of these are important examples of rural vernacular farmsteads. The other is a unique two-storied thatched dwelling, which at some stage of its life may have been raised from a single storey.

These three vernacular structures share the following characteristics: they face south; they have a protruding windbreak to their front façade; they are constructed of clay over limestone; they are thatched in the traditional sliced method using Oaten straw; two have substantial wattle fire canopies and they are roughly the same width but vary in length.

They nestle into the landscape of this narrow winding road and are only visible when one arrives at them. Two of these structures have been refurbished in the last decade and are excellent examples of what can be achieved by sensitive reuse. The fate of the third structure is uncertain.

That two of these structures were refurbished is due to the following:

– A willing owner who appreciates the potential benefits of an old vernacular structure.

– They are protected structures within FCC RPS.

– FCC now has a Conservation Officer who encourages and gives valuable advice on the refurbishment of such structures, accompanied by a new conservation grant system.

– Department of Environment and local government grants are available for the re-thatching of dwellings (only).

– The local non-governmental organisation (NGO) known as the Thatched Cottage Preservation Society of Fingal who constantly monitor the current stock of thatch giving advice and hands-on help to owners.

– The continuing availability of experienced thatchers.

The demolition of a thatched dwelling in Rush in 1998. The streetscape of Rush has lost in excess of sixty percent of its vernacular architecture over the past three decades. Not only are sound structures being allowed to be demolished but there is no effort being made to recycle good material such as the limestone which often finds its way to landfill.

Vernacular furniture

The vernacular structures and, in particular, dwellings had to have furniture, just as today's houses are kitted out with the necessities which make for comfortable living. While the basic piece of furniture for any house is a chair, there were many other essential pieces of furniture which were characteristic of the vernacular dwelling. Some furniture types, which were popular during the 18th, 19th and 20th century, were: Stools and Chairs; Dressers; Settlebeds; Tables; Beds; Cradles. Small furnishings included candle boxes, spoon racks, baskets and pictures.

A chicken coop, from vernacular dwelling, Rush.

In the thatched house in Rush restored by the author in 1996 the interior was furnished with all the above listed vernacular furniture.

The purpose of this survey was to identify vernacular structures in the field so it is impossible to quantify the extent to which vernacular furniture exists within individual structures. It was possible to gain access to some disused vernacular structures within the Fingal region. It appears that some original furniture still exists intact. This is partly due to the fact that these structures have not been occupied for some time.

An extremely rare vernacular chair (left) was identified in a dwelling near Ballyboughal and this is certainly a one-off chair; constructed of ash it resembles the design of a hedge chair.

An interesting feature found in vernacular dwellings in the townlands west of Balbriggan is what can only be described as a stone table. This table, found just inside the main entrance of dwellings, was for resting pails of water which the low temperature of the limestone table kept cool. Three examples of this feature were identified.

It is only through further surveys of dwellings that the extent to which original vernacular furniture exists can be quantified.

From the thatched dwelling at Skerries Road, Rush restored in 1996: top left, hearth fireplace; above, bedroom showing various furnishings; left, hearth room showing table and settlebed.

Farmsteads & Outbuildings

Throughout Fingal farmsteads appear in many different forms. Fingal is an area well-known for its intensive market gardening, centered around Rush, Lusk, Loughshinny and Skerries. As one moves inland and westward, cattle and sheep rearing become more widespread and tillage decreases. Farm buildings adhere to the basic characteristics of being almost entirely gabled along the eastern coast of Fingal, becoming hipped and half-hipped as one moves inland.

Location and age of vernacular structures are interesting in that structures located near quarries are constructed entirely of limestone with a clay wall plate used for the positioning and securing of roof timbers. In a good percentage of vernacular structures located in Rush, Loughshinny, Skerries and some rural locations there is evidence of older clay-built structures which predate quarrying.

In rural areas clay, or mud as it is often referred to, was used as the main construction material for walls. This walling material was often constructed upon a foundation of limestone which can be up to three or four feet in height.

Thatched farmstead at Carnhill, near Loughshinny. This 'Courtyard' farmyard was recently restored and is in use as a dwelling. It is a worthy example of what can be achieved in the reuse of vernacular farmstead.

A slated vernacular farmstead dwelling and associated outbuildings at Balrickard, near Balbriggan is a good surviving example of a two-storied slated farmstead with various corrugated outbuildings. While a good percentage of vernacular structures are thatched or corrugated or both, there are some examples of vernacular buildings which are slated and such buildings deserve the same protection as their equally impressive thatched counterparts.

Farmyard Layouts

Farmyards in Fingal have several different layouts. Three of these farmyard forms can be classified as follows: Parallel Farmyard, Linear Courtyard Farmyard and Courtyard Farmyard.

Parallel Farmyard

This type of farmyard is comprised of farm dwelling and outbuildings. The farmstead is usually situated across a lane or narrow road which enables both farmstead and main outbuilding to form a facing, parallel relationship.

The layout of an important vernacular farm complex, which can be classified as a 'Linear Courtyard' in the townland of Balrickard.

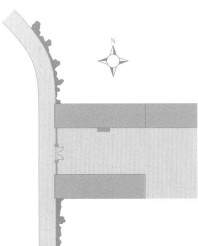

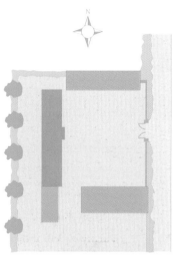

The layout of an important vernacular farm complex which can be classified as a 'Courtyard' farmyard in the townland of Balrickard.

Linear Courtyard Farmyard

This type of farmyard has the outbuilding as a continuation of the main farmstead in a linear form. A fine example of this type of farmstead was the thatched dwelling and linear attached outbuilding on the Skerries Road, Rush. The house was sold and subsequently restored in 1996. While the main dwelling still exists, the linear outbuilding was recently removed to allow access to the rear.

Courtyard Farmyard

A popular layout is the 'Courtyard' where the farm or main dwelling forms one side of a rectangular enclosure and several building of varying functions form the other sides. An interesting cluster of farmyards occurs in the townland of Balrickard, where three substantial vernacular farmyards are sited. While the dwelling of one of these farmyards has recently been demolished, still surviving are two rare examples of intact farmyards – a courtyard and a linear courtyard. Despite these vernacular structures being constructed close to the brow of a hill, they are entirely unobtrusive upon the landscape and, indeed, are only visible when you actually arrive alongside them.

This cast iron water pump of square profile, located at the cluster of farmyards in Balrickard, was the source of water for the inhabitants of the townland.

Left: a vernacular farm dwelling demolished since first surveyed in 1993. Fingal is still losing important vernacular farm dwellings through neglect and demolition. The vernacular outbuildings, shown below, of this 'Courtyard' farm have survived and add to the impressive cluster of substantial farm complexes at Balrickard.

Above: the visually impressive setting and grouping of different functional roof types of one of the vernacular farms.

Left: the vernacular doorway of the demolished dwelling featured above.

Above: vernacular outbuilding which forms the northern side of the 'Courtyard' farm complex at Balrickard.

Left: a two-storied farmstead situated near Garristown which was derelict and then demolished. In an era when farming is rapidly changing and diversification is the 'buzzword', the restoration and reuse of certain farm buildings could provide additional farm income for farmers and their families.

Outbuildings

Vernacular structures in rural areas usually have one or more outbuildings, depending on the various needs of the occupants. Outbuildings have fared badly in the overall picture of vernacular architecture, not only in Fingal but across Ireland also.

For example, despite the stock of previously mentioned thatched dwellings, very few thatched outbuildings exist. This is because the current stock of thatched dwellings were afforded both protection and grant assistance for re-thatching. There is no funding available for the re-thatching of outbuildings. In consequence, where they exist it is with a corrugated roof over the original thatched roof.

Above: a ruinous outbuilding in the townland of Pluckhimin, near Garristown.

A rare example of a courtyard farmstead with all structures, including the main dwelling, having corrugated iron roofs over their original thatch exists in the townland of Folkstown Little, near Balbriggan. Another example of a thatched outbuilding with a corrugated roof over its original thatched roof, complete with un-milled timbers, exists in the townland of Dermotstown, also near Balbriggan. The importance of these historic thatched roofs as examples of rare vernacular architecture

Below: farmstead outbuildings with all roofs corrugated over thatch at Folkstown, near Balbriggan.

cannot be overstated and as such they should be at least afforded the protection of inclusion within FCC RPS.

Most vernacular outbuildings are no longer used for what they were constructed, so encouragement by way of specific planning policies to enable imaginary and sensitive reuse of these building could ensure their survival into the future.

Above: Damastown outbuilding with (right) detail of doorway and (left) interior with bundle of straw rope hanging from un-milled, pegged ash rafters.

Forges

The work of the blacksmith took place within specially built forges. These forges of vernacular origin were an important and necessary part of both rural and urban-based communities in days past when there was considerable reliance on the horse. The blacksmith and his craft had a special place in communities; his work not only combined great strength and finesse but included skills that were vital to an agricultural-based society. Agricultural farming methods have changed dramatically over the past five decades and there are almost no working forges left within Fingal.

An important forge (pictured right) exists within the townland of Dallyhaysy, near Balbriggan. The structure's thatched roof still exists beneath the gray corrugated iron roof. This structure is possibly the only surviving thatched forge within the Fingal area. There are five intact forges left within Fingal County Council's administrative area – only one, situated near Donabate, is a protected structure.

Just as there are examples of formal and vernacular dwellings there is also the same diversity of formally designed forges and the traditional, or vernacular, forge which was as varied as each regional dialect. Some forges were constructed of neatly dressed stone and with a superbly crafted limestone doorway in the shape of a horseshoe complete with the traditional seven nail holes. This doorway was almost always constructed in the gable end of the structure, situated perpendicular to the road. The characteristics of a vernacular constructed forge were slightly different in that no formally dressed door in the shape of the horseshoe existed; the vernacular forge doorway consisted of a simply constructed double doors to allow for every eventuality.

The vernacular forge was constructed of locally sourced materials and may have either been roofed in thatch or of slate or, in the case of County Clare, Liscannor stone.

Above: a vernacular forge near Portmarnock, the door imitates a horseshoe.

Below: blacksmith Dick Lacey shoes a horse at his forge in the townland of Dallyhaysy on the Naul/Balbriggan road, circa 1940s.

Above: a forged iron gate bears the blacksmith's name – 'Maguire' – on the centre vertical bar, now gone due to road widening.

Below: carvings on rear of a headstone on blacksmith's grave in Naul graveyard, dated 1972.

In Fingal, the two previously described types of forge existed alongside an additional type. This was of vernacular origin but attempted to replicate the formal horseshoe type by constructing its doorway out of locally sourced red brick, imitating the shape of a horseshoe and painted black.

The remaining four vernacular structures that are forges within the administrative area of Fingal County Council should be placed upon the Record of Protected Structures. Surely the addition of these four important structures to FCC RPS can be achieved for the benefit of the heritage of the area? Additionally, these structures could be reused in a sustainable way and in so doing make a positive contribution to the vernacular architecture of the rural landscape of Fingal.

The Blacksmith

Up to the late 1950s and in some cases even later, nearly every village, town or parish had its own blacksmith and forge. Forge, by definition, refers to 'a blacksmith's workshop' and a blacksmith is defined as 'a person who repairs and makes things out of iron'. The Irish blacksmith performed a variety of tasks, from the repairing and sharpening of farm implements to the forging of ornate but functional farm gates. In fact, if one were to list all the tasks performed by the blacksmith it would include the following: repairing agricultural implements; shoeing wheels; making gates and railings; shoeing horses and donkeys; and the odd curing of warts and pulling of teeth! Forges were almost always sited at the sides of roads or at crossroads. They were great meeting places and a hub of activity.

The Blacksmith's Tools

Most of the tools in the blacksmith's forge were made by him. The only exceptions were items such as anvils, vices and the large bellows which fanned the furnace. Each blacksmith also had a distinctive way of marking his creations, for example, a forged iron farm gate might have a certain decorative scroll or, in some cases, the blacksmith's name would be stamped into the centre vertical bar.

The Blacksmith's tools – anvil and bellows.

Forged Iron Gates

Above, and opposite page: a selection of forged iron gates from around the Fingal area.

An important task performed by the local blacksmith was the making and repairing of forged iron farm and entrance gates. Field gates were often unique and variations occurred not only from county to county but from townland to townland. While some evidence exists to suggest that wooden gates were in use, the serious lack of trees in the Irish landscape from the 1700s onwards leads us to believe that forged iron was the preferred type of gate.

The function of any farm gate was to allow access to the field but, at the same time, to allow for livestock to be kept within or without. Forged iron gates were often hung between two stout pillars. This allowed for the secure hanging of these gates which were quite heavy. The pillars appear to come in two forms – either cylindrical or square – and in Fingal were mainly constructed of either random limestone or hand-cut dressed limestone. The field gate had to be able to swing forward like a fire crane, directly on its heel; this heel slotted into a stone socket at ground level. The simple handle with a curled end was designed to slide into a slot in the limestone pillar.

While gates varied from townland to townland, and from blacksmith to blacksmith, some similarities did exist. A popular design of farm gate throughout the Fingal area was of horizontal gradating bars with a semi circular support bar. Almost all of this type of gate has six horizontal bars of gradually decreasing gap size, from top bar to bottom, supported by a semi circular bar from heel to heel. One elaborate version of this field gate is located in the townland of Mooretown, near Oldtown and is a truly remarkable piece of work. No forged iron gates appear on the FCC RPS.

Cast Iron Pumps

A total of thirty-three cast iron water pump sites were identified by the author within the Fingal area. There are distinctly three types of cast iron water pump: the square profile, the round profile and the smaller round profile.

Of the thirty-three pump sites identified, two with dressed limestone pump-surrounds have had the original cast iron pump removed. A total of twenty cast iron pumps are in perfect condition. The remaining eleven sites are in an imperfect condition – ie, some feature of the original pump is missing; most commonly the lid or the handle and in some cases both. The NIAH identified thirty-one cast iron pump sites in their 2001 survey. FCC have a total of two cast iron pump sites comprising of a total of three pumps placed on their RPS (one pump site has two pumps).

Left: this site at Donabate contains a smaller round profile and a square profile pump, and is listed on FCC RPS.

Right: this round profile pump is situated at Ring Commons.

Left: a small cast iron pump at Rush harbour.

Watermills & Windmills

The Mills of Fingal can be subdivided into two categories according to the elements that powered them, namely watermills and windmills.

The main purpose of a mill was to grind grain into flour, the main ingredient of various breads. Bread was and still is a significant part of people's diets. Mills were constructed in such a way that they used the renewable energy harnessed from water and wind – the ultimate in sustainability.

Watermills

Watermills in Ireland can be dated back many centuries – one that comes to mind is the remains of the horizontal mill on High Island, off the Galway coast, a truly remarkable monastic vernacular mill. Fingal is not blessed with an abundance of rivers but despite this there are a number of good examples of mills. The river Ward which glides through Swords once had three impressive vernacular mills – the last surviving was demolished in 2001 to make way for apartments which are yet to be built. Such was the alteration to the river and surrounding landscape during the construction of watermills that their associated weirs still survive long after the main structures have been demolished. A good example of this is the surviving weir at Bridge Street, Swords where a heron can be seen fishing regularly for pinkins and minnow.

The river which flows through the village of Ballyboughal appears to have only one vernacular mill, situated at Grace Dieu, an historic area where once stood a medieval nunnery. This mill has its wooden interior workings still intact and a two-storied dwelling close by appears to be the miller's house. Another interesting watermill exists in the Naul village and on closer inspection it is apparent that it was once a smaller mill with a steep pitched roof. This almost certainly suggests that it was thatched at one time and is possibly pre-1700s. This ruinous mill has recently been turned into apartments and is an example of the reuse of a disused vernacular mill.

By far the most impressive vernacular mill is sited in the townland of Killossery, near Rolestown. It is reputed to date to the 1600s which would make one of the oldest vernacular structures within Fingal. In recent years the mill has become vacant and only remains in its present condition due to the corrugated iron roof which was placed over

Right: Grace Dieu, a vernacular mill, situated at Ballyboughal and, below, a view of the machinery.

Left: Killossery vernacular Mill complex. A protected structure (yet it is being allowed to decay) and one of the most important surviving corrugated iron-over-thatch group of buildings found within the Fingal region.

the original thatched roof in the 1930s. Its survival hangs in the balance and it is a protected structure.

Windmills

There are at least seven windmills identified in this study. All are protected structures and five are in a ruinous condition. All of the windmills are circular in form and have an entrance door at the base and a window opening higher up in the structure. Until recently all of Fingal's stock of windmills was in a ruinous condition. The reconstruction of both vernacular windmills in Skerries as a tourist attraction is a perfect example of the value that vernacular structures can be to a community if sensitively reused.

Images of the windmill at Skerries: below, as it was circa 1900; centre, before restoration; far right, the restored mill.

Limekilns

Limekilns, as their name suggests, were used for the making of lime for use in building vernacular structures and for spreading on the land to enrich the soil. A limekiln is basically a tall square limestone structure usually built into the side of a hill or into the side of a quarry. It was important to build them near quarries, which allows for easy access to the main ingredient, limestone. Limekilns are essentially hollowed structures with a cylindrical brick-lined flue. The limekiln was packed with crushed lime and either turf or wood to allow for the continual burning of the crushed lime, which over a period of a few days would become lime powder.

There are three limekilns contained within the FCC RPS but, since only seven remain in total in Fingal, surely they could all be placed on the list? There are two very good examples surviving within the villages of the Naul and Oldtown. These are the only surviving limekilns within urban areas and as such will experience pressure from development. Limekilns are an important part of Fingal's vernacular industrial and agricultural heritage. To place these two limekilns within FCC RPS would be a major step towards preserving these unique structures.

Left: the limekiln at Oldtown and, inset, detail of flue interior.

Holy Wells & Household Wells

A detailed study of any ordinance survey map will reveal the locations of Holy Wells. These wells are denoted by the very words 'Holy Well' in oldstyle typeface. Some wells have vernacular structures on top which were built at some period of their existence to protect them and allow easy access. The Holy Well on Well Road, Swords has an association with Saint Columb who founded a monastery in Swords in the sixth century. While the structure of the well has gone through some changes within the past decade, it still stands relatively intact and this is due to the care taken by a local historical group. The well is no longer in use but retains its hand-forged iron gate, which has links to the nearby forge, the remains of which were demolished in 2005. While all of the Holy Wells (totalling fifty or so) are National Monuments and are listed in the FCC RPS, a good number of wells are on private land and have fared badly (see Case Study No. 6 on page 47). Would it be too much to hope that some financial package could be put together to encourage landholders to maintain and fence off such important structures?

Ordinary household wells were just that. When a rural vernacular dwelling or farmstead was built, an important and much needed feature was a freshwater well. Sometimes a

well might have existed already near the site or, in some cases, a well would be bored. This deep cylindrical well was usually lined with limestone. A cover or capping was put on for safety.

Left: St Columb's Well, Swords and, right, a household well at Adamstown.

Boathouse

Despite Fingal's lengthy coastline only one vernacular boathouse appears to be still in existence. Situated at Loughshinny harbour, it has some characteristics of a more formal structure designed by an architect but it is believed that it is in fact vernacular. This structure appears on FCC RPS and also in the NIAH survey of 2001.

A detached single storey gabled-fronted boathouse, it was built around 1880. It is built of locally sourced limestone possibly from Milverton Quarry. This boathouse has one square headed double door opening in its east-facing gable. It has limestone coping to both its gables, this allows for the protection of each roof gable from prevailing winds and is also a decorative feature. Its windows are segmented and have original wooden shutters.

The structure would have been used for the storage or repair of fishing boats. It is now disused since its last owner passed away. Finding practical uses for this unique structure will determine its future, for it is only through imaginative reuse that its survival can be assured.

Vernacular structures & Planning issues

"Vernacular buildings should not be preserved for their aesthetic and ecological value alone. They should be viewed as a resource and an asset, not a liability for planners and developers. Other countries have devoted considerable resources to preserving their vernacular building tradition and the policies followed have reaped tangible rewards by fostering viable tourist and craft industries. In Ireland, an effective system of grants and incentives coupled with ready advice would go a long way towards safeguarding our vernacular heritage for the future".
(Dublin Heritage Group, Vernacular Buildings of East Fingal. 1993. Santry Print Ltd).

It appears that, regardless of the policy contained within FCC's Development Plan, planning permission is being given to demolish some fine examples of vernacular architecture. The Kitchenstown example (Case Study 5) makes a good case for a comprehensive survey to be carried out by FCC, leading to the listing of worthy structures. This would be the first step in the preservation of a rich vernacular heritage which, as each year passes, is being gradually eroded. While this study has highlighted only six examples, there are countless more. As great effort is put into the preservation of the remaining stock of thatched dwellings, little or no effort is being made to protect other more worthy examples of vernacular architecture. While FCC have included within their most recent RPS a more detailed description of its protected structures, it should adopt a more comprehensive listing, complete with photographs.

Right: the longest vernacular structure in Fingal, near Balbriggan.

Case Study 1. A Listing Inaccuracy

Thatched Dwelling, Drogheda Road, Lusk. Corduff (part of) FCC No. 273. Four bay single-storey thatched dwelling in gated vernacular complex.

This vernacular complex (FCC RPS Site No. 273, NIAH reference number: 11323014) is a vernacular structure of local, regional and national importance. This structure's last inhabitant was an elderly woman in her nineties who died in the year 2001. The structure does not have any toilet facilities or running water within its walls but it does have electricity and a phone. A planning application lodged with FCC in November 2004 (reference number F04A/1599) sought planning permission for the demolition of part of this vernacular complex to gain access to the lands to the rear to facilitate the building of a nursing home. The planning application did not state that the structure was a protected structure and was deemed invalid one week after it was lodged with FCC. Subsequent research by the author revealed that while FCC were sure that this important vernacular structure was a protected structure its identification on their development plan maps proved difficult for the following reason. Each protected structure is afforded a reference number and this number appears on the relevant map as close as possible if not upon the structure. In this case the reference number appeared some considerable distance away, in fact about half-a-mile, in a field with no other recognisable structure on site. When this became apparent to FCC they wrote to the developer-owner and proposed listing the vernacular structure. This vernacular structure has a wattle fire canopy complete with bressamers, a spy window, blade pegged roof timbers, some original vernacular furniture and a personal association with the patriot Thomas Ashe whose oil painting of this very structure, painted in the early 1900s, used to hang in the hallway until its removal following the death of the previous owner. Over the past four years this vernacular dwelling has steadily begun to return to the earth from which it was constructed.

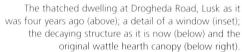

The thatched dwelling at Drogheda Road, Lusk as it was four years ago (above); a detail of a window (inset); the decaying structure as it is now (below) and the original wattle hearth canopy (below right).

Case Study 2. Planning Permission Granted for Demolition within an Architectural Conservation Area

Vernacular Dwellings, Lower Main Street, Rush.

This appeared to be an important smugglers style vernacular dwelling with a corrugated iron roof and which would have had a thatched roof originally. This case study highlights the inconsistency between FCC policy on vernacular architecture and actual development control decisions. This group of buildings on Lower Main Street, Rush was identified by this survey but not identified by either FCC or the NIAH as having any significant architectural merit. For the purpose of this study a visual assessment was made, adhering to the same format as used by the NIAH. This concluded that this group of buildings is an important contribution to the vernacular streetscape of Lower Main Street, Rush, an area once characterised by a high percentage of thatched roofs (see photo below). It was

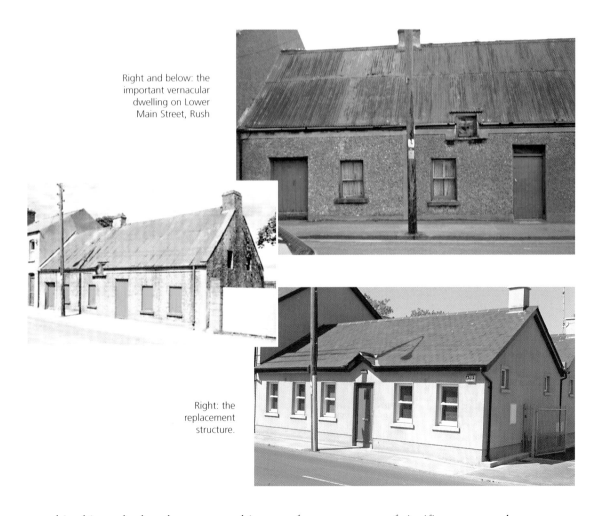

Right and below: the important vernacular dwelling on Lower Main Street, Rush

Right: the replacement structure.

noted in this study that the corrugated iron roof structure was of significant vernacular value based purely on the visual assessment of its south facing façade and east gable. A planning application to demolish this structure and replace it with duplex apartments was lodged with FCC in November 2004 (register reference number: FO4A/1656). A decision made on the 25th of January 2005 was to allow the demolition of these important vernacular structures within a proposed Architectural Conservation Area (ACA) in the FCC DDP 2005-2011. The structure appeared to be sound; its replacement, a mock-vernacular, is a hideous attempt to satisfy some planning official.

Case Study 3.   Lack of enforcement

Thatched dwelling, Drogheda Road, Lusk. Corduff Hall. FCC RPS number 272. Four Bay single-storey, semi-detached thatched dwelling.

This vernacular semi detached dwelling is listed in FCC DDP as a protected structure and was formerly a List 2 category structure in the Development Plan 1996-2004. The structure has been unoccupied for at least ten years. The owner carried out works on this structure in the summer of 2004. The works comprised of the removal of the hipped, thatched roof and its replacement with a gabled, slated roof. Under the Planning and Development Act 2000, Section IV, it is an offence to carry out any works without first obtaining planning permission. Under PDA Part iv S.57.2, an owner occupier of a protected structure may make a written request to the planning authority in order to obtain a declaration from the relevant local authority in order to carry out certain works (examples of such works could be the replacement of sash windows or a temporary covering of thatched roof with, lets say, corrugated iron in order to address any deterioration). It is the opinion of this study that the removal of a thatched roof from a protected structure is an offence under PDA IV s. 58.1. To date no action has been taken by FCC.

Above: the dwelling before removal of the thatched roof.

Left: with thatched roof and hipped gable removed.

Case Study 4. Planning Permission Granted for Demolition of a Thatched Structure

If it is the policy of FCC to protect vernacular architecture and their settings, then the question must be asked: "why was an important vernacular structure in the shadow of the impressive ecclesiastical remains in the town of Lusk allowed to be demolished and replaced with a structure that is incompatible with this architecturally rich setting?" In 1997, planning permission was granted for the demolition and replacement of a dwelling on Barrack Road, Lusk (planning reference number F97B/0447). The demolished structure was not only a vernacular structure in an important setting but also an original thatched dwelling. Research for this study has uncovered that the inspection carried out by the planning officer failed to identify that this vernacular structure had a thatched roof beneath its corrugated asbestos roof.

Left: before demolition;

Below: the replacement structure.

Case Study 5. Planning Permission Granted for Demolition of a Thatched Structure

This case study highlights a decision made by a professional planning officer. The decision was made in favour of the demolition and I quote the competent planner: "The existing structure, although of some architectural merit, is not listed for conservation or preservation".

The farmstead, at Kitchenstown, near the Naul, still stands today and a replacement dwelling stands alongside it. This hipped substantial vernacular farmstead has similar characteristics to the Mayglass farmstead of County Wexford. The Mayglass farmstead was restored by the Heritage Council because of its heritage values. This vernacular structure is one of the largest hipped and surviving farmsteads in Fingal. Once again it highlights the importance of carrying out a complete survey followed by the listing of important structures. At time of going to print this structure still stands. In September 2007 Fingal County Council had employed Brendan P Lynch to carry out this survey.

Left: the farmstead at Kitchenstown with replacement dwelling alongside.

Case Study 6. The covering over of a Holy Well – a national monument and protected structure

The Holy Well at Balrothery, known locally as Saint Bridget's Well, is a National Monument (Ref Number: DU 005-05707) and is also a protected structure contained within FCC RPS. A recent development has resulted in the alteration of the setting of the well beyond all recognition: in excess of fifteen feet of soil has been purposely heaped over this holy well and, as if that were not enough, the beautiful venerated tree (a rarity in Fingal) was chopped down.

Left: the well as it was; below left: the venerated elder tree; below: the well as it is now.

Appendix I
Breakdown of Vernacular Sites

The breakdown of vernacular sites as identified in a study compiled by the author in the spring of 2005. It should be noted that this is not an exhaustive study, the actual number is reckoned to be considerably higher.

Dwellings	462
Outbuildings	23
Forge	5
Commercial	42
Cast Iron Water Pumps	33
Wrought Iron Forged Gates	20
Windmills	6
Limekilns	5
Holy Wells	1
Village Halls	1
Boathouses	1
Total	**600**

Appendix II

Vernacular Architecture versus Formal Architecture

based on Barry O'Reilly's "Living under thatch", p. 13, 2004.
(some additions by this author)

	Vernacular Architecture	Formal Architecture
Builder	From immediate locality, name rarely known.	Can vary but almost always by an architect and can be documented with research .
Owner	Farmer, labourer, smuggler, thatcher, fisherman. Often the builder.	Includes wealthy individuals and professionals, rarely the builder.
Scale	Relatively small scale.	Often much larger.
Costs	Relatively low.	Usually higher.
Design	Drawn down from tradition, simple shapes.	Often designed professionally, can involve complex shapes.
Inspiration	Traditional.	Influenced by architectural styles.
Climate & siting layout	Very carefully considered, often one room deep, back wall to the prevailing wind and small windows.	Can vary, usually two rooms or more deep.
Materials	Local materials, also reuse of such materials as ships' timbers. Traditional.	Materials often out-sourced.
Survival	Heavily rural.	Greater proportion are urban.
Dating	Rarely datable.	Usually a date known.
Protection	Few protected by law.	Proportionately more protected.

List of Illustrations

All photographs and illustrations are by Brendan P Lynch unless otherwise stated.

Bibliography

Buchanan, Ronald H., Thatch and Thatching in North-East Ireland, Gwerin, 1 (1957).

Danaher, Kevin, Ireland's Traditional Houses, 1975.

Dublin Heritage Group, Vernacular Buildings of East Fingal, Santry Print Ltd 1993.

Fingal County Council, Planning File, F99A/0608, November 1999.

FCC Development Plan, 1999-2004.

FCC Development Plan, 2005-2011.

Gailey, Alan, Rural Houses of Northern Ireland, Donald Publishers 1984.

Gore-Grimes, John, Key Issues in Planning and Environmental Law.

Mullane, F., The Heritage of Ireland, Vernacular Architecture, Collins Press 2000.

Oxford English Dictionary, Edited by Catherine Soanes.

Planning and Development Act, 2000.

UNESCO, Charter on the Built Vernacular Heritage, Mexico, 1999.

About the Author

Brendan P Lynch

Born in 1968, Brendan grew up in the village of Ballyboughal. From an early age he cycled the lanes and byways of Fingal, which helped to develop his appreciation and knowledge of the rich vernacular architecture of this area. He played violin from the age of twelve and learned the tunes from the older musicians. Brendan has recorded two solo albums of fiddle music which have received excellent reviews and he still tours and plays.

In 1987 Brendan suffered a severe farm accident which resulted in hospitalisation for eight months and involved reconstruction of his leg. Despite this he has regained good mobility. In 1993 he formed the Thatched Cottage Preservation Society of Fingal. Its main aim is to stop the decline of vernacular thatched structures. In 1996 Brendan bought two thatched dwellings in Rush which were in a dilapidated state. They are now restored and used as dwellings, and both are protected structures.

In 2001 Brendan embarked on a full time four-year undergraduate course in Town Planning. He graduated with honours in the summer of 2005. His thesis forms the basis of this book.

Brendan is also an accomplished artist and holds at least one solo exhibition each year. He continues to share his love of music and architecture through his work as a musician and artist and remains committed to the conservation of the rich architectural heritage not only of Fingal but of all of Ireland.

Damastown Farmstead

a poem by Brendan P Lynch

Why must we demolish wipe away as if we are so ashamed of it
What did it do wrong, what did it do to us
It only stood us well and housed our ancestors
For century after century
And just as light appeared over the hilltop
And into the hearth and with that flick of
That light switch all was revealed

The dull and darkness of our past that hath lain
Just beneath the surface ready to be scratched like
That itch that never went away
Well it will soon be gone
And with it all the many centuries of what made
Us rich and rare cultural people
With sense of place

And music and song and tradition
The settle bed, the dresser, the half door, the vernacular chair
Yes that one-off chair that gleamed like the new light bulb
That chair will be as fascinating to future generations as
The light bulb was to the past

The friendliness the warmth oh that warmth
Oh I am sorry and apologise for my generation that has
Turned its back on you and to the false God of money, power,
quick fix solutions, pollution and ill health
Oh I am sorry

The poem was inspired by the overnight demolition of one of the most intact vernacular farmsteads in Fingal. The chair and one outbuilding are all that survive.